By The Sea

Sea

M. L. Borges

The beauty and mystery

Of the ocean, fills our lives

With wonders, vast beyond

Our imagination.

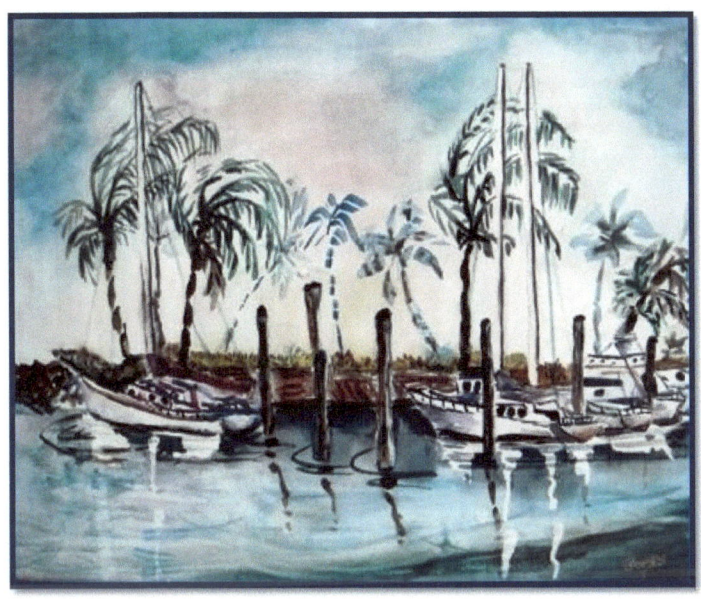

The boats sit in the harbor
patiently waiting for their
time to sail off into the sea.

The dock sits and waits
for its coming patrons
whose clock follows only
the patterns of the sea.

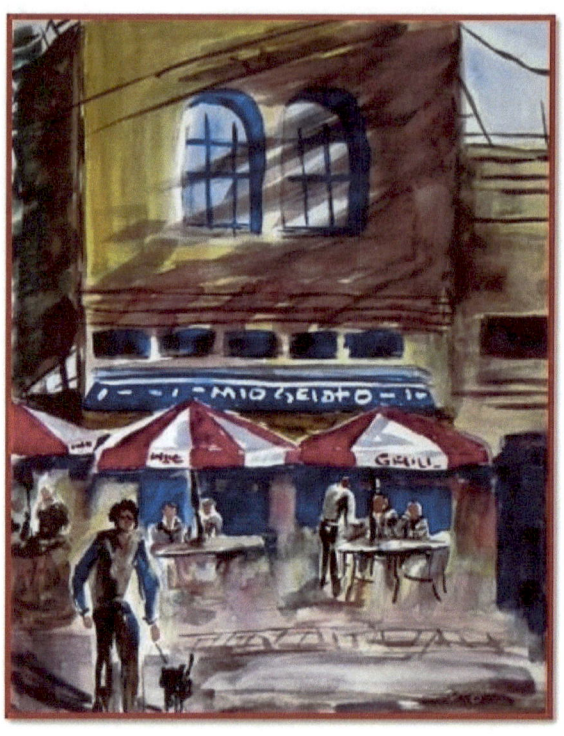

You and me with our dog
makes three as we
sit by the beautiful sea.

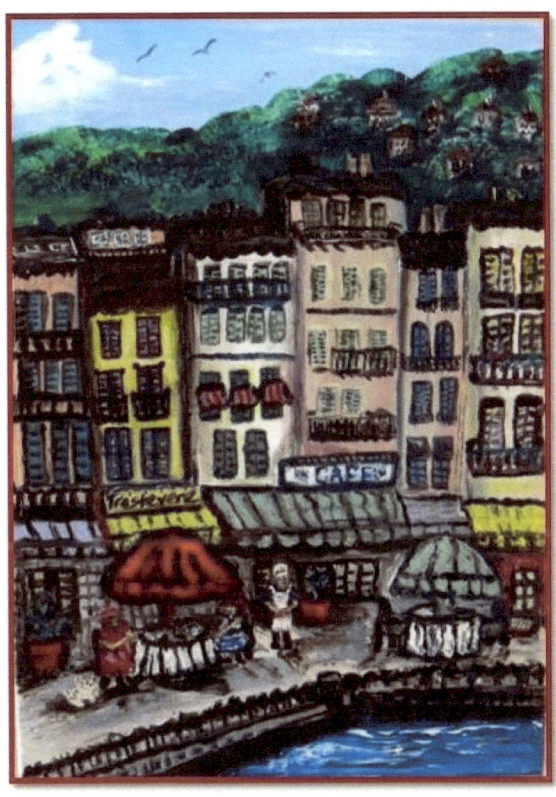

The ocean has a
vicarious emotion unique
to the constant motion of
the waves.

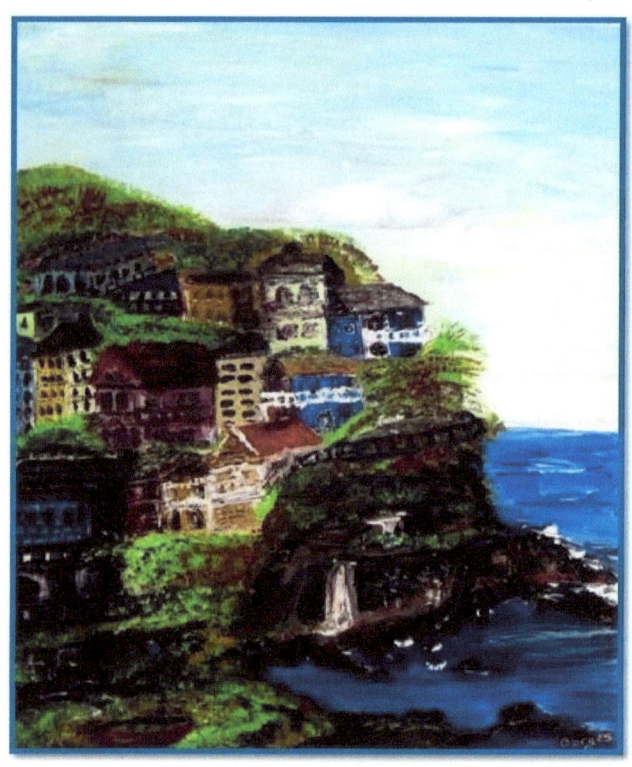

Pasta, amore, beauty
and the sea, what
a combination of
glory to be seen.

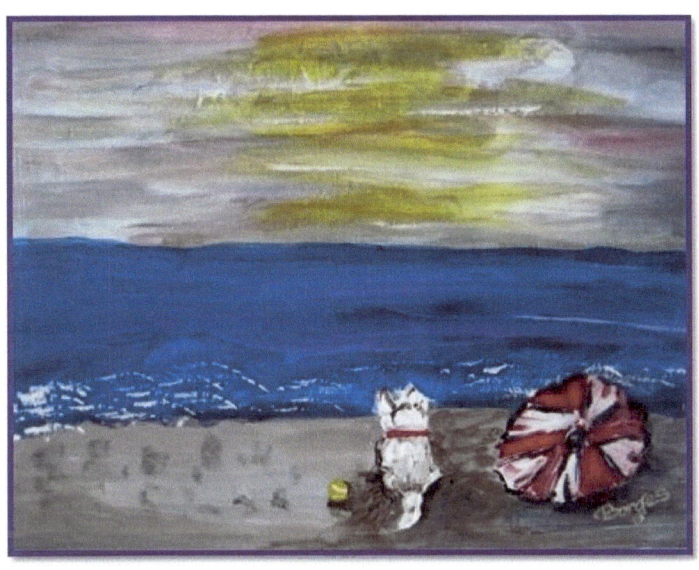

My day is made
when we go to
dogs beach to play.

Sun, sand, running
along the shoreline of the sea
chasing a ball with my
pal and me.

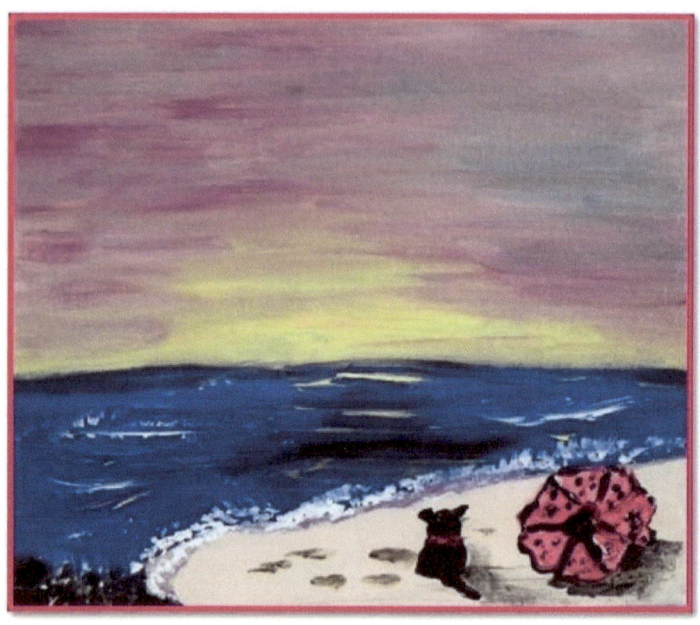

The beach is a place of
solitude where I can set
my spirit free and relax.

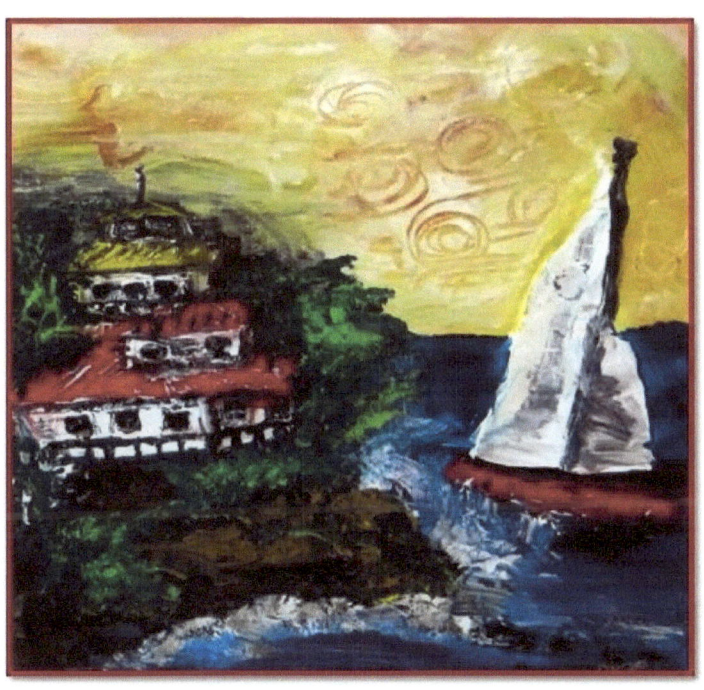

Our sailboat glides on
the sea around the
island it rides along
with the gusty breeze.

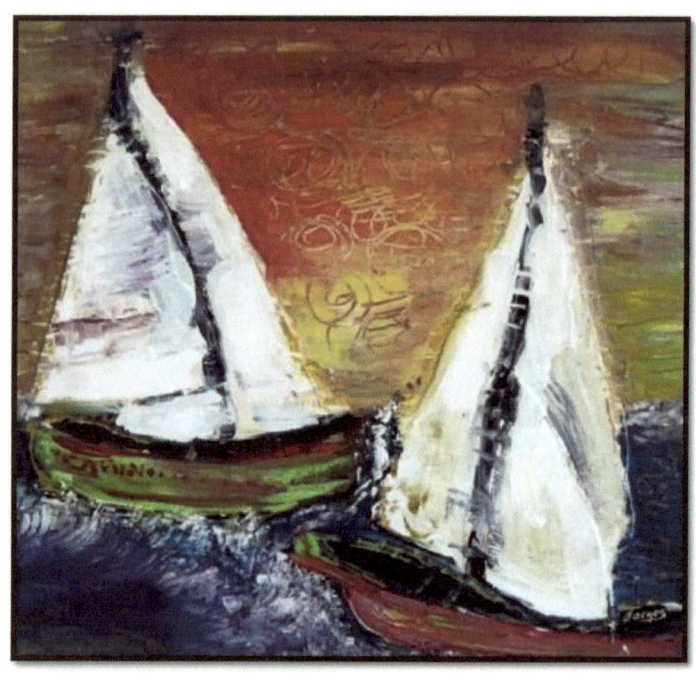

Sailing the sea we
travel along the
roaring coast and
with the wind we soar.

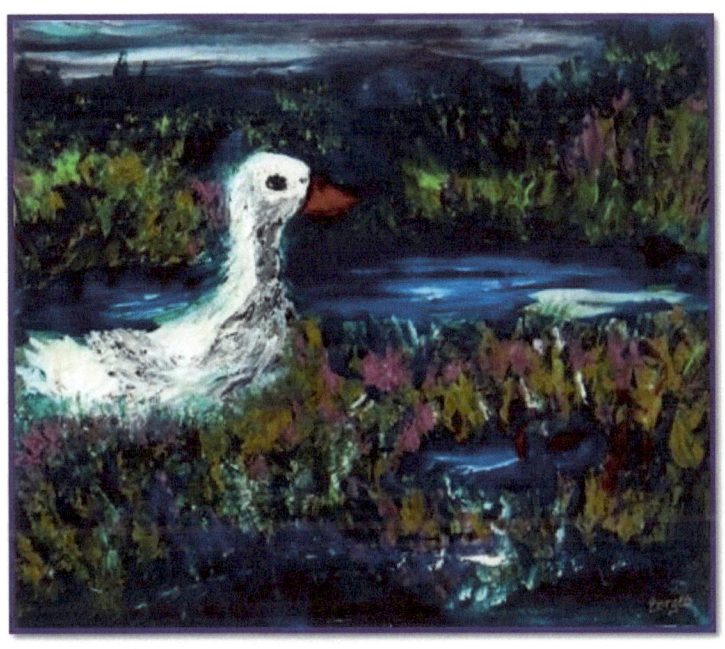

Just to be in a
moment by the sea
brings a sense of
well-being and peace.

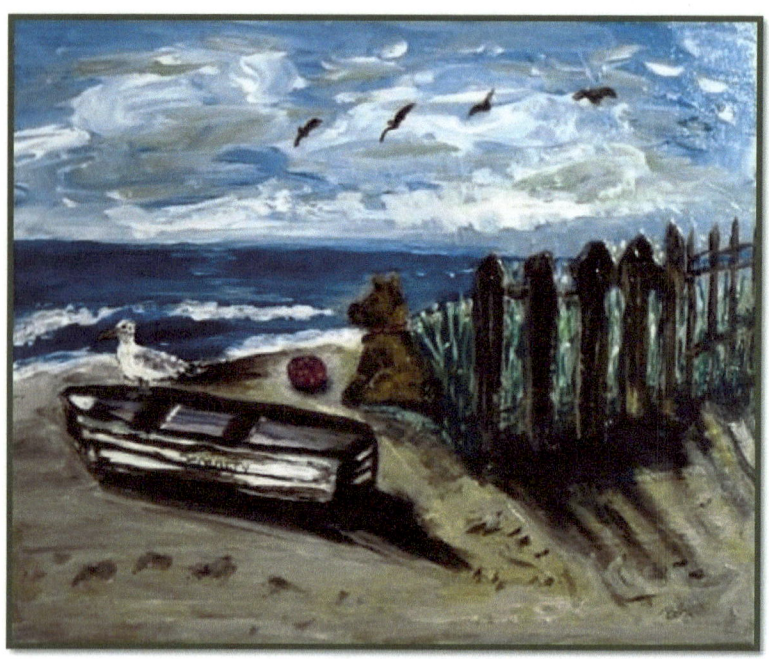

There is no better place to be
than at the sea with
my ball and beach friends.

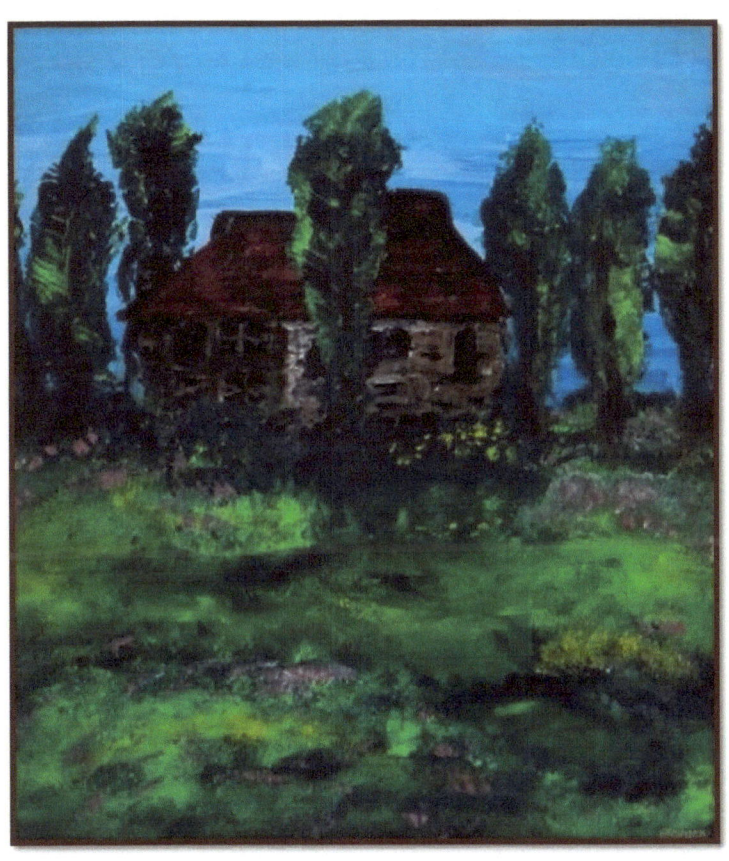

The Villa by the sea
is a special place to be.

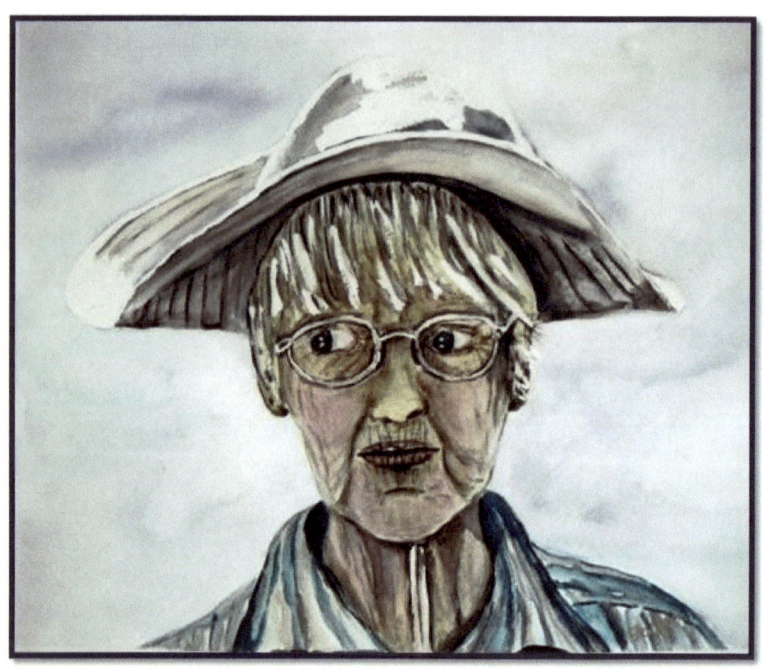

The gardener is always
ready to tend to her plants
and swim in the beauty of
the sea.

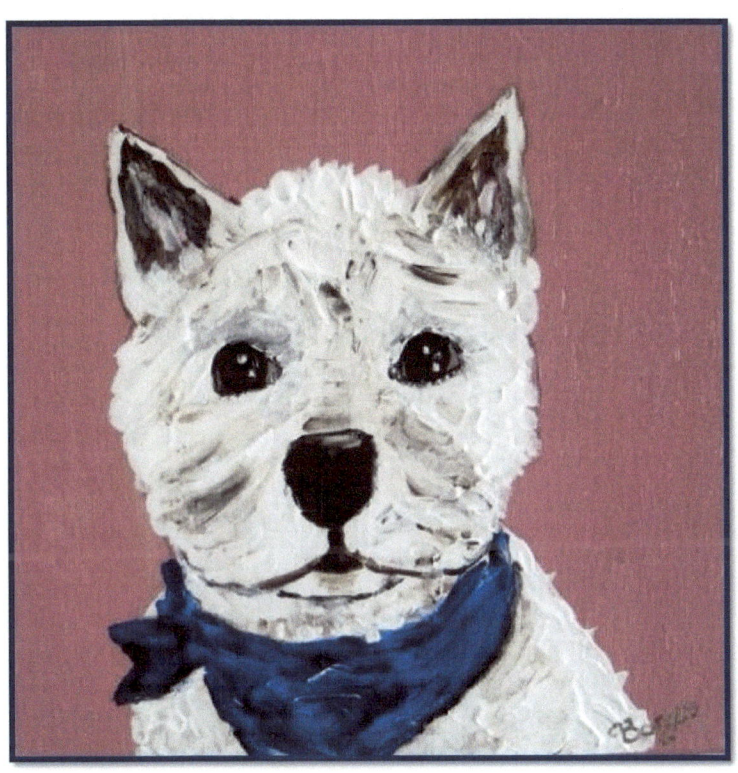

There is a time for
everything but the
best time is my
beach time.

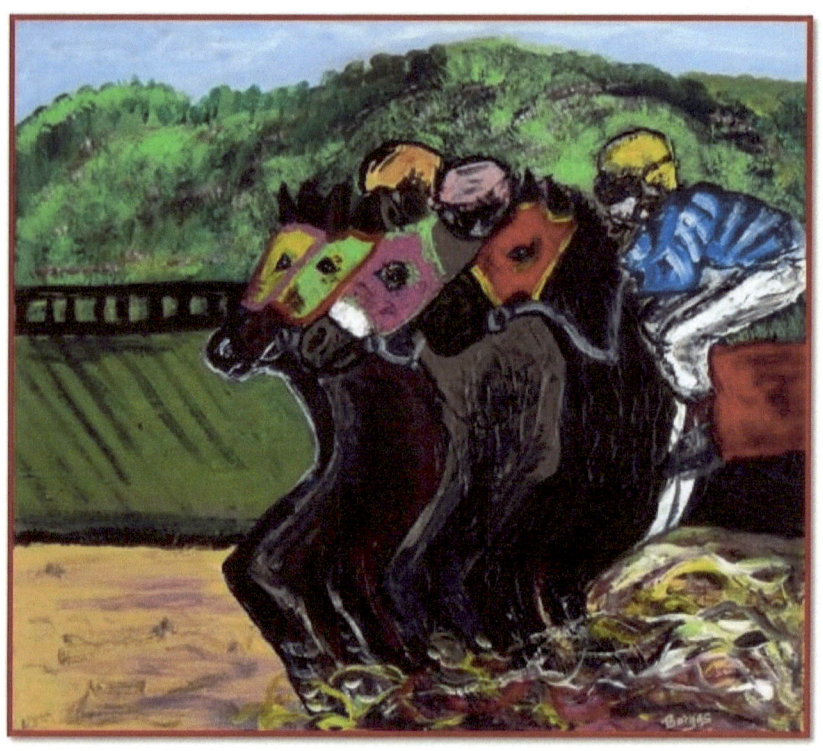

Air fuels the engine
the sea brings the breeze
and the beautiful horses
run in full motion and elegance.

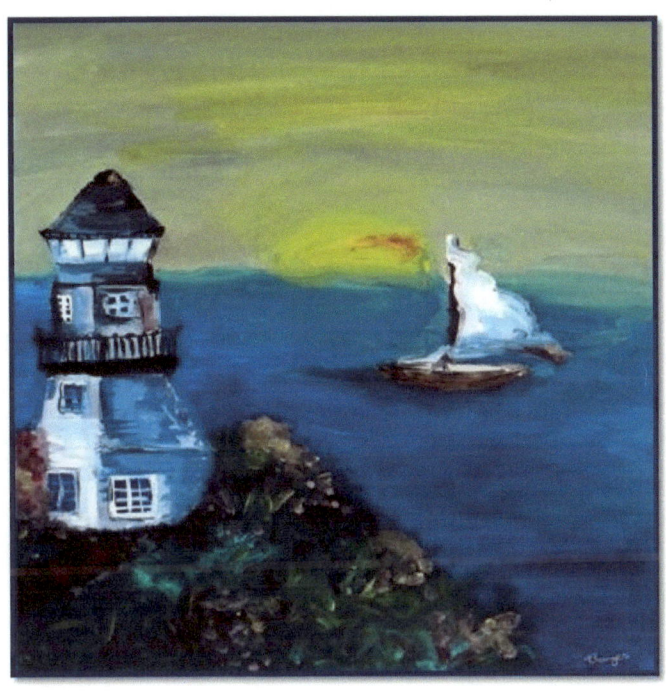

The mysterious wondering
of a lighthouse has been
used by many to create
captivating stories.

Sailing around the bay
the sea a calm whisper of gray
watching the sunset
for another day.

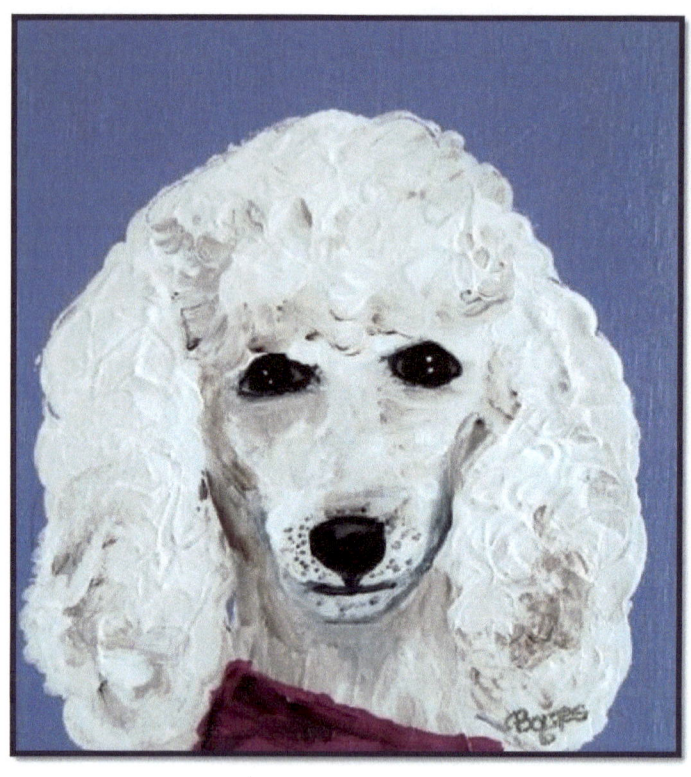

All that time at
the doggie doodle shop
fussing and mussing with
my hair when all I want to do
is run on the beach, swim and
roll around in the sand.

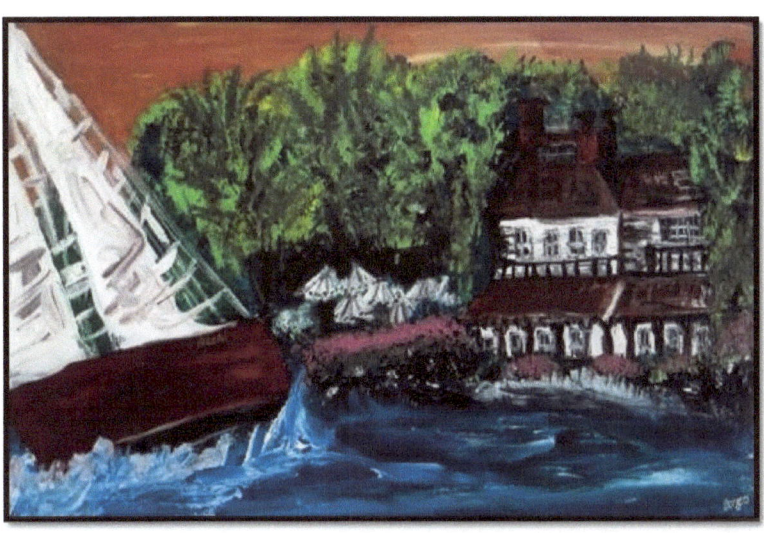

From the west to the east
the sea rolls around
creating visions of wonder
in all its pathways.

The wind at work
has unpredictable quirks
but when it is full
the sails soar with delight.

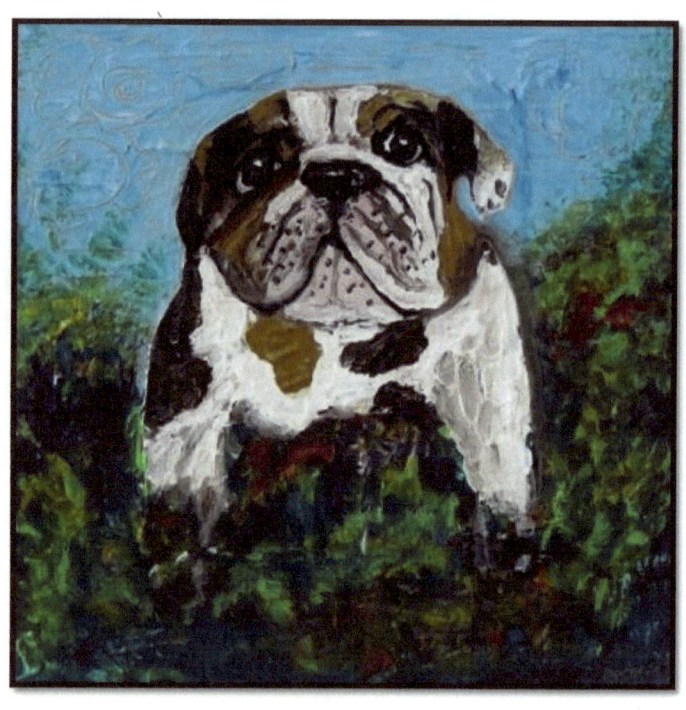

Dogs love the sea
where they are able
to run free to chase and play
all the happy moments
of their day.

My love of the sea
is only surpassed by
my love for food.

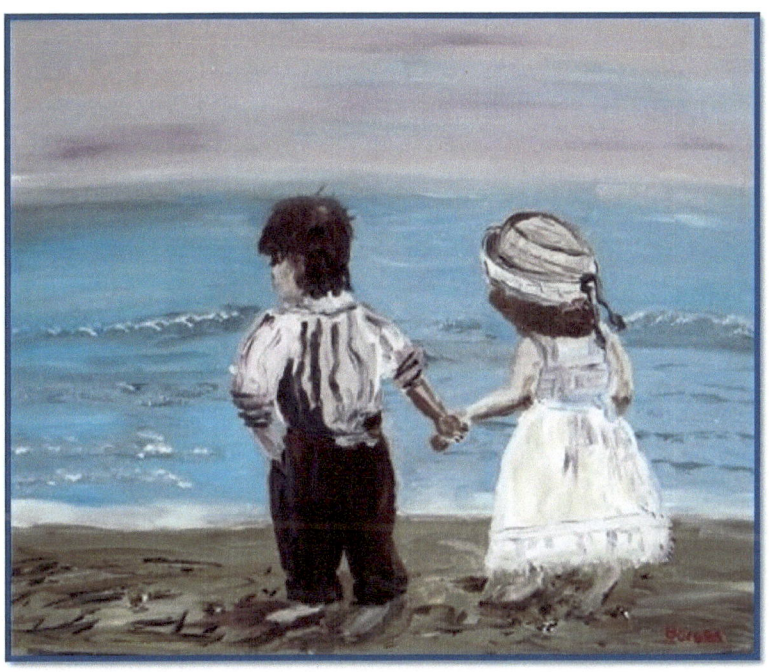

By the sea my honey
and me, hand in hand,
we walk along the sand.

The calming movement of
the sea along with the restless
ocean breeze gently caresses me
creating a soothing trance which
lulls me to a place of peace.

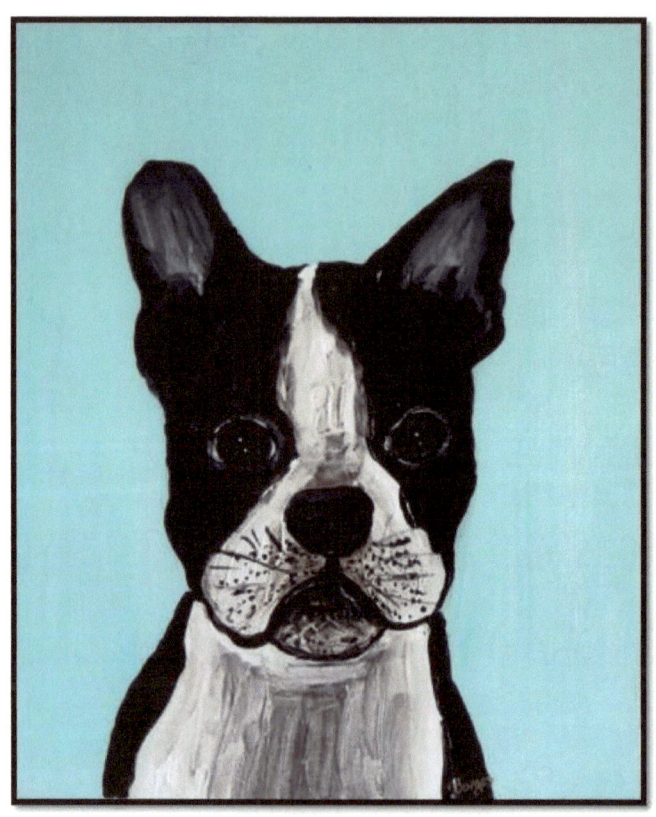

When I sit by the sea
my heart fills with glee
and each peaceful
moment sets my spirit free.

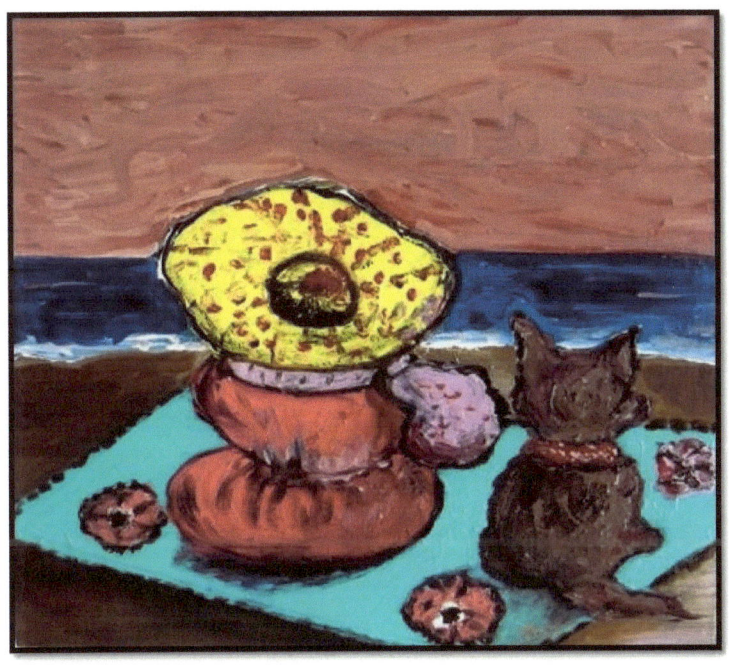

The sun is out full and bright
creating a wonderful day to
sit and enjoy the rhythmic
sound of the ocean as it roars.

The waves swirl in a
circular fusion that fall
back into themselves and floats
again on the surface of the sea.

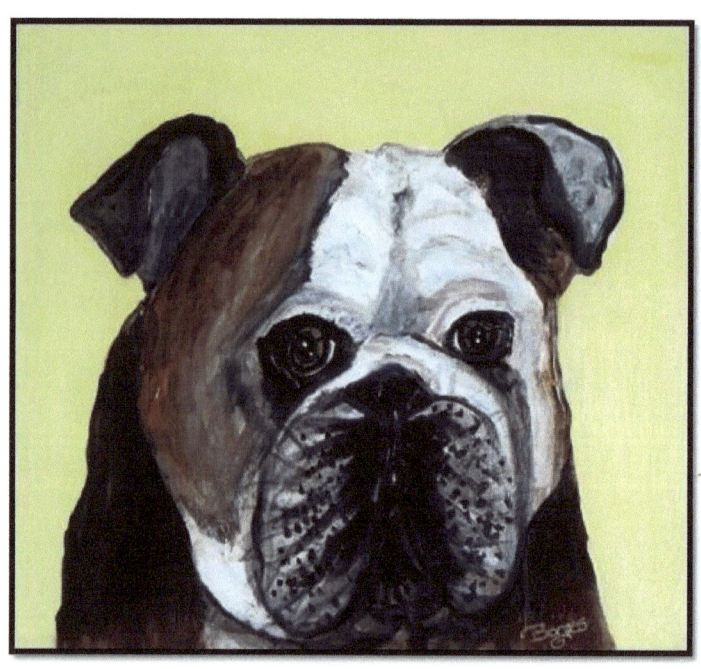

Take me out to the park by
the beach and watch my
body spark into action
with ball chasing energy
following my natural attraction.

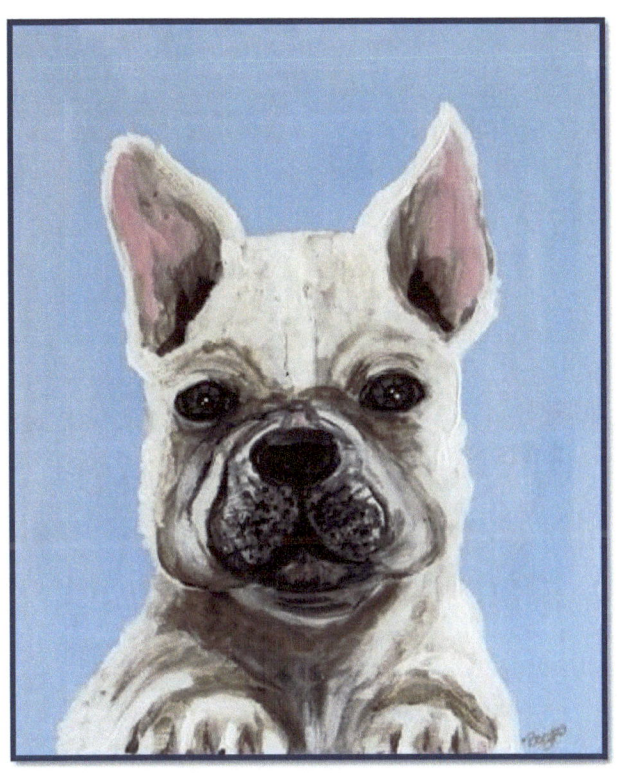

J'aime la mer which
for me is better than
an éclair but siding the same
with a filet mignon.

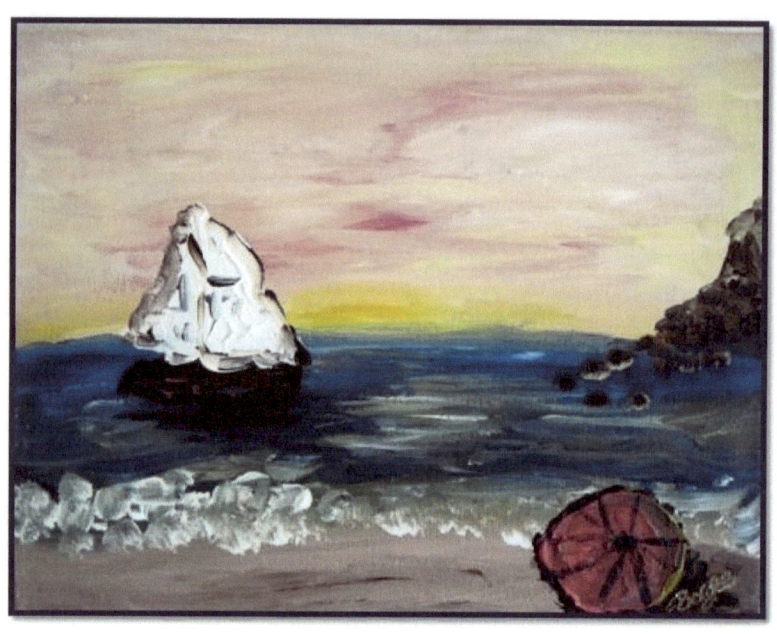

The ship is out at sea
where it goes is a mystery to me,
will it come back or melt into the
ocean that is vast with
endless motions.

The sky surrounds us
with sunlight while
the wind gives us the
power to roll along
the beautiful sea.

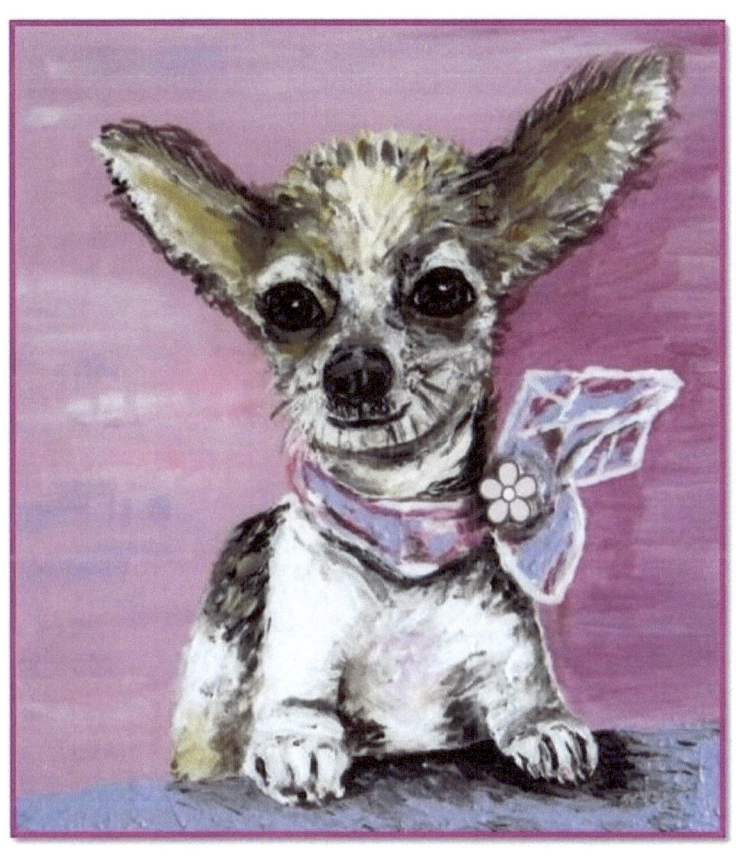

The beach is mighty pretty
right here from my window
this way I don't get sand on
my beautiful nails.

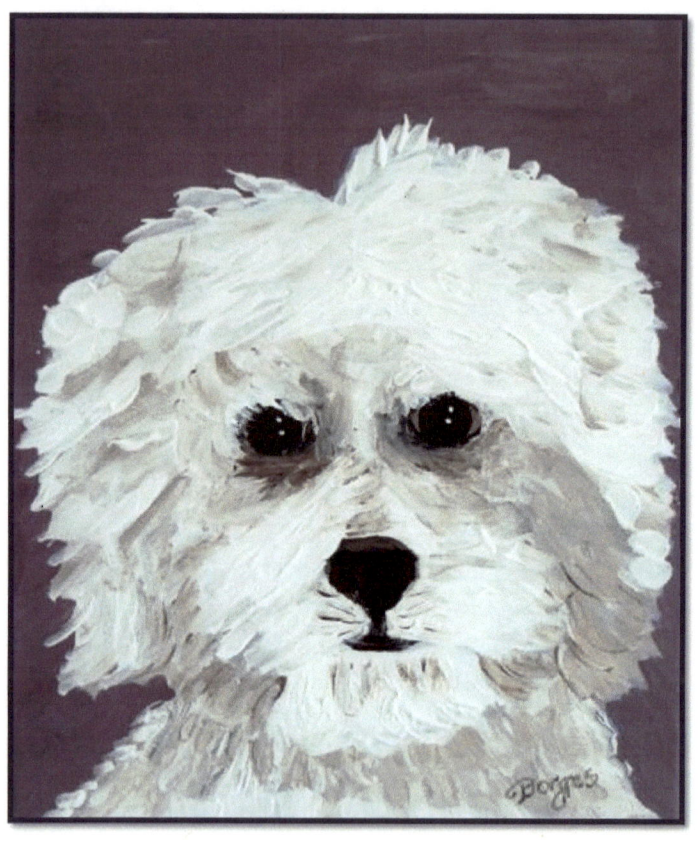

My favorite place to go
is to the beach with my
ball so that I can chase
the day away.

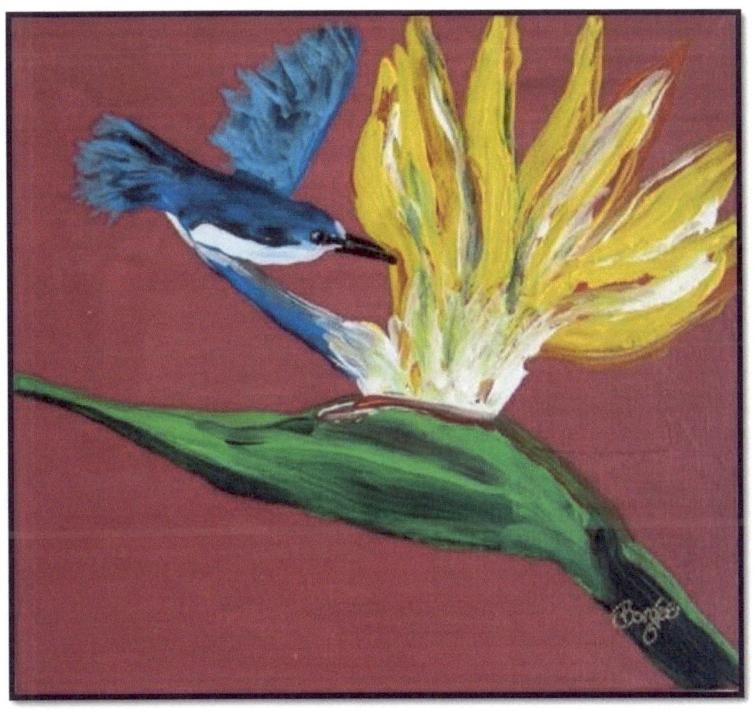

Humming around to
all the birds of paradise
breathing the fresh ocean air
while spreading flower power
and singing throughout my day.

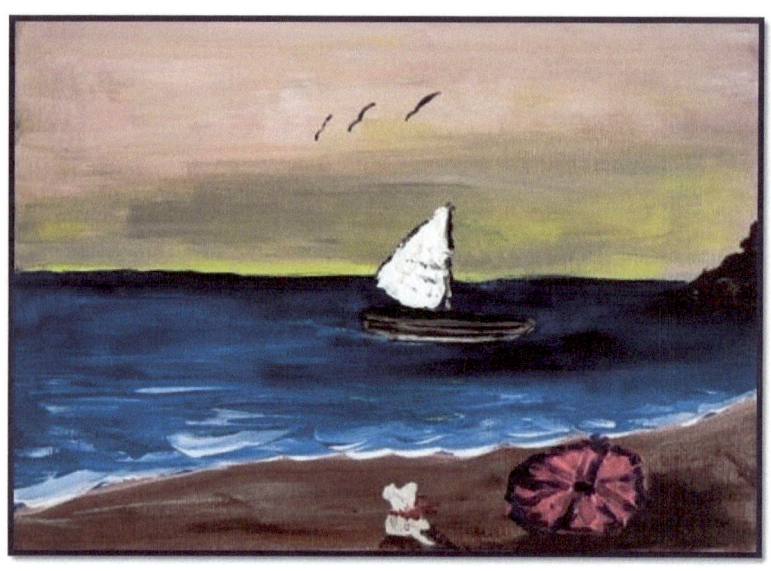

As I sit by the sea
watching the boats sail by
I wonder what it is like to
swim under the water and
live in a world that we
can only dream about.

The sea is a conundrum
of amazing proportions as
it is filled with a vast world
of aquatic treasures
and wonders.

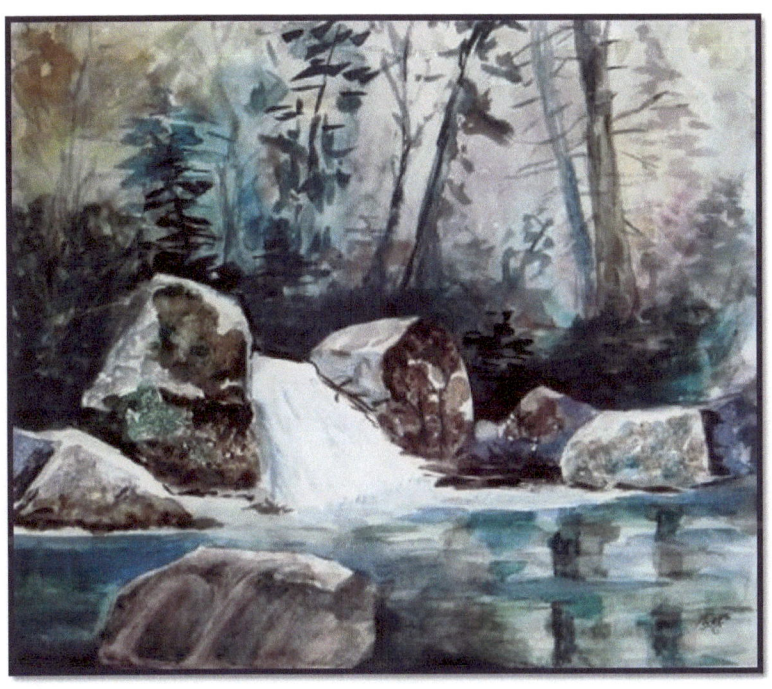

The waters from the ocean
channel into waterways on
the land, around the trees, through
cascading falls creating a network
that zigzags in contorted movements
like a train traveling through
a wavy mountain.

About the Author & Artist

M. L. Borges

Art is a wonder in itself and we see it every day, presented around us, through glorious colors, moments, feelings, and expressions. Art has been a part of my life from the moment I could hold a pencil. I started with animated characters, mostly inspired by the cartoons I loved to watch as a child. From there, I learned to work with oils and filled my free days, from school, with art classes. When I was in college, I had the pleasure of taking classes from well-known artists, such as: Wayne Thiebaud, Roy De Forest, and Manuel Neri. Today, I continue to take art classes that inspire me to learn. As with any craft, it's an educational journey.

My favorite mediums are acrylics, watercolor, and mixed media. My love for animals, the ocean, sailing, and nature are the focus for the settings I paint. I love all the mediums I work with because art is an expression that reads in many languages.

Painting is the visual interpretation and writing is the written picture. Both visual artists and writers paint, one with a brush and the other with words. For me, I have been writing for as many years as painting because one craft inspires the other. I believe we have a common bond that holds both mediums together, in a mix called creativity. It's by the sharing of our creative energies that we get the most rewards.